Table of Content

I0470480

Foreword

Most people point to the age-old practice of marking livestock as the genesis of the modern day concept of branding. If only that were the case. During those more self-reliant times, attaching a mark or family name to a product was a highly symbolic gesture; one that not only proclaimed ownership, but also ascribed one's reputation and personal commitment to a product's value.

Today's common notion of branding is a corporate, cosmetic undertaking that is detached from people's personal character. Taking hold in the 20th century with the advent of mass-produced products and broadcast media, it is image-driven and message-obsessed. Unfortunately, this mindset persists despite the radical changes in the prevailing context and conditions of today's economy.

Prior to the industrial age, consumers and producers gathered to exchange value directly in an open forum or market. Customers often looked to others in the community for information and guidance, and so word of mouth and trust were the chief determinants of success. One's standing in the community had to be earned by offering products of real and lasting value.

During the industrial age, the nature of the marketplace changed. Consumers relocated from small communities to jobs in cities and towns, where they relied on retailers for food, clothing and household products. This coincided with the advent of mass production and mass consumption and ushered in an arm's length, transactional mindset and orientation. Marketers became more concerned with sales and promotion of goods, and less with providing distinctive value as a means to building ongoing relationships. The focus was on driving down unit costs through economies of scale, and using distribution and mass marketing techniques to find customers for their excess production of goods and services. Branding was their chief means of differentiating and controlling the distribution of those homogenous offerings.

Well, it's d j vu all over again. Rapid technological advancements have brought us back to the future. Today's post-industrial age, like pre-industrial times, is a fragmented marketplace of communities of like-minded people looking for distinctive value. It's overflowing with an abundance of products, along with skeptical people who

increasingly rely on others in their "communities" for information and guidance. Value and trust are, once again, the principal determinants of success.

Despite this fact, most businesses persist in the folly of branding. The pernicious cognitive pull of this powerful industrial-age concept, along with the ecosystem that evolved to perpetuate it, is holding back marketing thought and organizational action. Make no mistake: People are wasting a lot of time and money on branding. The marketplace has moved on, but most organizations have refused to go along for the ride. And, like fish with water, most are completely unaware of it.

The Danish philosopher Søren Kierkegaard wrote, "Concepts, like individuals, have their histories and are just as incapable of withstanding the ravages of time as are individuals." The industrial-age idea of branding will ultimately die its timely death, but I wouldn't wait. Instead, open your eyes to today's marketplace realities, embrace the valuable concepts in this insightful ebook, and create an Awakened Brand. By doing so, you'll create value and trust, and the mutually beneficial, long-term relationships that are at the heart of every successful enterprise.

Tom Asacker
Author of A Clear Eye for Branding

The Business of Belief:
How the World's Best Marketers, Designers, Salespeople, Coaches, Fundraisers, Educators, Entrepreneurs and Other Leaders Get Us to Believe

Author Bio

Virginie Glaenzer is a sales and marketing executive with over 25 years experience in the U.S. and international markets. A seasoned business expert in SAAS and new technologies, she has been instrumental in the founding of two software start-ups and is an established authority in social media, mobile, and digital marketing.

Through the development and execution of highly successful integrated communication channel plans and platforms, she is a leader in traditional and non-traditional marketing strategies with a strong emphasis on social media and mobile. She is devoted to sharing her passion for growth hacking and agile marketing strategies.

Virginie holds a master's degree from HEC Paris (Ecole des Hautes Etudes Commerciales), one of France's top three business schools.

After spending 17 years in Silicon Valley, Virginie moved in 2012 to New York City with her husband and three daughters.

VIRGINIE GLAENZER

Executive Vice President of Marketing & Customer Experience

Introduction

Your brand's value is based on more than just an eye-catching logo and whether your product beats the competition's product. Today, a brand's value is often defined by its self-awareness, true authenticity, and relevancy. If a brand isn't in complete synergy with the consumers' tastes, sensibilities, and desires, there is more to worry about than a logo. Consumers are looking for brands that will impact their lives in tangible, positive, and lasting ways.

It's common to assume we are rational decision makers, yet it's no secret that the most successful brands tap into our emotions. A number of bestselling books, including Nobel Prize winner, Daniel Kahneman's, Thinking, Fast and Slow have challenged the assumption that we are always rational beings, showing that a vast majority of our decisions are based on emotions and intuition, and that most of our decisions are made in seconds. Malcolm Gladwell explains in Blink: The Power of Thinking Without Thinking "that our mental processes often work with very little information. This intuitive decision- making can help us do what we'd never be able to manage without it. It's knowing without knowing – irrationality at its best."

The fact is that we are driven by our emotions, particularly our negative emotions. We tend to emphasize the negative instead of the positive thanks to our caveman ancestors. Being aware of and avoiding danger is a critical survival skill. Because of this, consumers are more likely to make choices based on their need to avoid a negative experience rather than their desire to have a positive experience.

Yet, tapping into positive emotions can help your brand connect to consumers and thereby transform your brand. Research shows that people tend to live longer, more fulfilling lives when they're happy. Therefore, positive emotions , while not critical for our caveman ancestors, are the key to engaging today's consumers.

Companies that can convert their product's features into positive benefits for the consumer are able to tap into this higher level of consciousness. Companies that don't examine the meaning and emotions behind the value their product provides to customers will miss out on a wonderful opportunity to take their brand to the next level and become an Awakened Brand.

"Logic will get you from A to B. Imagination will take you everywhere."

ALBERT EINSTEIN

Are You Part of The Consciousness Revolution?

Gluten-free, reducetarian, and Citizen science. Crowdsourcing, quantum think, green energy, and global warming.

Healthy living, reducing your carbon footprint, crowdsourcing, the sharing economy, quantum mechanics, the law of attraction, going green, climate change and corporate responsibility.

If you think these movements and theories have nothing to do with your brand, think again. Welcome to the Consciousness Revolution.

You may have heard about the Consciousness Revolution. Author Dianne Collins calls it the "New Mainstream" or "The Consciousness Crowd." The Consciousness Revolution is not defined by age, income, political beliefs or geography, but by a new mindset, an expanded worldview and a higher-level of consciousness for humanity and all things affected by humankind. This movement is largely untapped by marketers, and thus represents a new opportunity for companies to engage with their customers in a completely new way.

People who are part of the Consciousness Revolution look beyond labels to a brand's connection with a broader mission. Today, consumers are attracted to brands that strive to improve our environment and society.

This movement has been quietly going on in the background for years and it's starting to gain momentum. In the last five years, there has been a number of new trends: Healthy living, reducing your carbon footprint, crowdsourcing, the sharing economy, quantum mechanics, the law of attraction, going green, climate change and corporate responsibility, gluten-free, reducetarian, citizen science and quantum think.

These trends are not random.

They are all connected to something bigger. Something is happening that is profoundly changing our society and could change the way we market our brands.

This profound change will lead us to create an Awakened Brand.

In fact, you may even be part of this Consciousness Revolution. Have you started to pay more attention to what you eat, are you concerned about climate change and energy consumption, do you think social media is a more reliable source of information than news media organizations and corporations? Then you are probably part of the Consciousness Revolution.

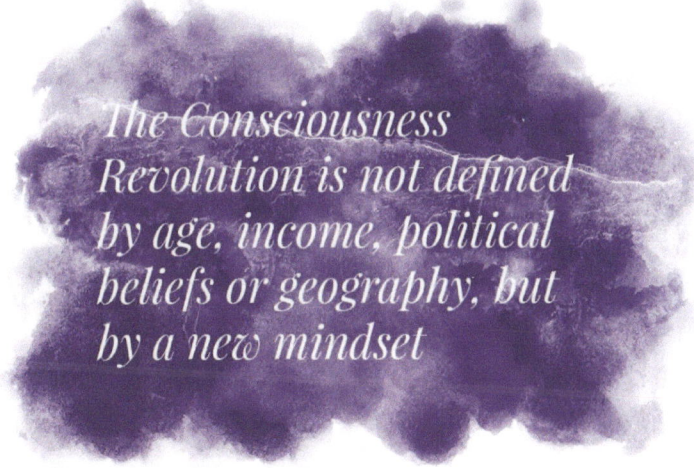

The Consciousness Revolution is not defined by age, income, political beliefs or geography, but by a new mindset

What We Eat

Have you recently decided to pay closer attention to what you eat and drink for dietary or ethical reasons?

NBC's Today Show nutrition expert and founder of Nourish Snacks Joy Bauer says: "There's been a rise in popularity of eating 'clean,' wholesome foods and the trend is only growing." She adds, "There's been a real movement towards organic, locally sourced, and humanely raised produce and meats."

According to a study published in the Journal of the American Dietetic Association, about 61.5% of Americans reported consulting the nutrition facts panel before purchasing packaged food. Consumers are also becoming more concerned about food sustainability. Two-thirds of Americans report that they have given "some thought" to whether the foods and beverages they purchase is produced in a sustainable

way. About four in ten (41%) consumers say they purchase foods and beverages that are advertised as "local." A slightly smaller percentage report buying foods and beverages at farmers markets (39%) and purchasing foods and beverages in recycled and/or recyclable packaging (38%).

Finally, the vast majority of Americans (94%) have given some thought to the amount of physical activity they get, with 61% reporting that they have given a lot of thought to the issue.

61.5%

of Americans reported consulting the
nutrition facts panel before purchasing
packaged food.

41%

of consumers purchase foods and
beverages that are advertised as "local".

38%

of consumers purchasing foods and
beverages in recycled and/or recyclable
packaging.

Where We Live

Are you concerned about climate change and how to reduce your energy consumption?

According to a 2014 New York Times/CBS News poll, more than half the American public says human behavior is causing global warming and climate change. This is the highest level of public concern ever recorded in the national U.S. poll.

There is overwhelming scientific consensus that climate change and global warming is caused by human behavior. Over 95% of climate scientists agree that the earth is warming and human activity is the cause.

We are seeing initiatives around the world like the Union of Concerned Scientists and the C40 Cities Climate Leadership Group (C40), a network of nearly 75 cities around the world that are taking measurable and scalable actions to reduce their carbon emissions. C40 also partners with the Clinton Climate Initiative and The World Bank to accelerate progress on combating the negative impacts of climate change.

Who We Trust

Do you think social media content is more reliable than a statement by an organization or the news media?

A recent survey by the Reputation Institute found that only 15% of people trusted what companies communicated in their advertisements and that 43% were unsure if goods and services were of a high quality. In his book, The New Influencers: A Marketer's Guide to the New Social Media, Paul Gillin talks about the impact social media has on brands. One of his key points is that 78% of consumers trust each other more than they trust advertisements.

As social media usage has becomes more widespread, consumers are using it to share their personal experiences with brands and products, as well as their experience with the company's customer service and purchasing processes. The Society for New Communications Research surveyed more than 300 consumers on how brand perceptions and purchasing behavior is increasingly influenced by their use of online tools and social media to read, research and share their customer care experiences in a study titled, "Exploring the Link Between Customer Care and Brand Reputation in the Age of Social Media."

According to the study, 81% believed that blogs, online rating systems, and discussion forums can give consumers a greater voice in customer service, but less than 33% believed that businesses take customers' opinions seriously.

15%

of people trusted what companies communicated in their advertisements

81%

believed that blogs, online rating systems, and discussion forums can give consumers a greater voice in customer service

43%

of people were unsure if goods and services were of a high quality.

78%

of consumers trust each other more than they trust advertisements.

The Last 50 Years of Revolutions

To better understand what's driving the Consciousness Revolution, let's look back at the last 50 years.

1950s - The Automobile Revolution: After the 1929 Stock Market Crash and World War II, the automobile revolution develops new infrastructure, which leads to "the suburban way of life" as well as the development of new cities across the country.

1960s - The Love & Civil Rights Revolution: Segregation, gender equality, and other political issues lead to minorities demanding more power while the younger generation questioned authority and their government, and rejected consumerist values.

1970s - The Computer Revolution: The first personal computer was introduce in 1975, laying the foundation of what will become the Internet and mobile revolution 20 years later. This created the opportunity for businesses to increase communications speed and simplifying business processes. 1970s was also the advent of the sustainability movement due to the gas crisis.

1980s - The Materialist Revolution: This decade is most associated with greed and consumerism perhaps, in part, because plastics technology lead to the increased production of mass products, and the frequency and size of business mergers and acquisitions hit new heights during this decade.

1990s - The Digital Revolution: This third industrial revolution resulted in everything analog, mechanical, and electronic being switched to digital technology. It changed the way businesses operated and the time it took to get products and ideas into the marketplace, and it started to lay the foundation for the Consciousness Revolution.

2000s - The Mobile & Social Media Revolution: Suddenly the world is smaller and consumers are able to connect and communicate with people all over the global. This globalization leads to political changes as well as the way businesses function, fundamentally changing consumers' expectations about their relationship with brands.

2010: The Beginning of The Consciousness Revolution

In 2010, we start to see the advent of the Consciousness Revolution as consumers begin to demand brands that are organic and responsible enabling them to thrive and connect emotionally to the product or service.

IT'S ORGANIC

Organic has two meanings: First our society is moving towards a natural, sustainable food chain. It also means that because of social media, knowledge and information about brands is growing and spreading naturally amongst consumers who love and vouch for brands.

IT'S THRIVING

We have the desire and the means to improve our society using technology and world knowledge that empowers us to thrive.

IT'S RESPONSIBLE

Our society is beginning to feel responsible for the current state of the planet: increasing pollution, decreasing natural resources and climate change. Consumers want to engage with companies that are socially and environmentally responsible.

EMOTIONALLY INTELLIGENT

Our society is recognizing that our decisions are not always based on data and facts but on our emotions and gut feelings.

The Consciousness Revolution is an opportunity for brands to feel more connected with consumers when they share similar beliefs. This leads to increased engagement with the brand, which then becomes an Awakened Brand.

Consumers begin to demand brands that are organic and responsible to enable them to thrive and emotionally connect.

Who is in the Consciousness Revolution?

The Consciousness Revolution unites a diverse group of people. This revolution isn't defined by gender, age, religion, or political views. These are people who want to feel connected to a broader mission. They want to change the world to make it more equitable and more sustainable. Here is a broad look at who is in the Consciousness Revolution.

WE ARE YOUNG

Yet we are changing the world.

TEDxTeen tells the story of many incredible young people changing the world.

Here are two examples.

At 15, Jack Andraka developed a promising new test for the early detection of pancreatic cancer and won the youth achievement Smithsonian American Ingenuity Award.

Kelvin Doe is a teenage engineering whiz kid living in Sierra Leone. He scoured the trash bins for spare parts, which he used to build batteries, generators, and transmitters to create his own radio station where he broadcasts news and plays music as DJ Focus.

WE ARE SENIOR

Yet we are embracing new values.

Although Conservative Catholic groups are alarmed by some of the Pope Francis's comments, this new pope is standing up for women's rights, gay rights, and the environment, and gaining popularity among all Americans, not just Catholics. According to a Pew Research Center survey, Pope Francis is rated favorably by 70% of all Americans, not just those who are religious.

Baby Boomers are embracing technology at a higher rate than Millennials, according to Chris O'Brien, former technology reporter at the San Jose Mercury News. Baby Boomers are tweeting, Facebooking, blogging, using iPods, and playing video games at a much higher level 9than ever before, according to O'Brien.

Baby Boomers may be more open to technology because online devices and gadgets can provide health and wellness support. "Recent advancements in technology and demand by baby boomers have increased the popularity for wellness devices," writes John Patrick Pullen in an article for Entrepreneur.

Meanwhile, Baby Boomers are responsible for most philanthropic giving, according to a report by Blackbaud. Boomers contribute 43% of all giving.

WE ARE THE 99 PERCENT

Yet we are thriving.

Humans of New York is a photo-blog and bestselling book featuring street portraits and interviews collected in New York City. Photographer Brandon Stanton started it in November 2010 and he has collected more than 6,000 portraits, more than 15 million Facebook followers, and more than 3.8 million Instagram followers.

Earlier this year, one of Stanton's portraits featured Vidal Chastanet, an eighth-grader at Mott Hall Bridges Academy in Brooklyn, N.Y. Vidal said his school principal Nydia Lopez was the most influential person in his life. The post, which immediately went viral on Facebook, was shared more than 145,000 times. Stanton contacted the school principal, and took photos of the teachers and students for a week. He and the principal decided to start a fundraising project on Indiegogo Life to send the students on a trip to visit Harvard University. Their goal was to raise $100,000. Instead they raised $1.4 million.

This is just one example of the power of crowdsourcing, which encourages the global exchange of information and ideas at lightening speeds. Crowdsourcing isn't just for individuals. Businesses are also using crowdsourcing to get input from multiple sources, both within their corporation and externally, to develop strategic solutions, find better ways to complete tasks, and produce better products.

This new culture of innovation, supported by crowdsourcing, allows for idea collaboration and technological innovation for the greater good for all. Further, in our increasingly connected world, crowdsourcing allows people from anywhere, and with any background, to give their input on a project.

Great examples of crowdsourcing includes Picnic Green Challenge - Ideas to save the planet, Open Ideo - Solve big challenges for social good, Eyeka, Idea Connection- Solve problems for monetary prizes, Crowd Spring - Crowdsource graphic design and logos, Quirky- Contribute to various phases of the product production process, or shop products created by the crowd, Ideaken - Collaborative crowdsourcing. Seek for solutions and solve problems,

Humanitarian Innovation Open innovation challenges to solve humanitarian problems and Young Foundation - Disruptive social innovation.

WE ARE THE 1%

Yet we are donating our wealth.

The wealthiest 400 Americans are worth over $2 trillion. Together, they own as much wealth as the bottom half of American households combined, according to a 2013 report by Charlie Rose, which ran on CBS's 60 Minutes.

Although we have seen increased resentment among the U.S. population towards the super rich, many of these rich people are donating staggering sums of money, in what is being called a "golden age of philanthropy."

Bill and Melinda Gates, and Warren Buffet are among the wealthiest donating huge sums of money to help solve some of the world's biggest problems. They started the Giving Pledge and invited the world's wealthiest individuals and families to commit to giving more than half of their wealth to philanthropic or charitable causes either during their lifetime or in their will.

WE ARE BUSINESS LEADERS

Yet we are sharing strategies for cultivating mindfulness and how it influences our decisions.

We are all busy, engaged people, pulled in many directions, looking for ways to cultivate mindfulness.

Mindfulness mediation was mainly done at spiritual retreats and in yoga centers, but now it is practiced in offices, schools, prisons, and even by the U.S. military. Although it's been around for decades, the mindfulness movement is being called a revolution. Advocates say it reduces anxiety and has spiritual benefits.

Corporate culture has taken to mindfulness training avidly: Harvard Business School, New York University Stern School of Business, and McDonough School of Business at Georgetown University now offer courses in mindfulness, perhaps because a large number of corporations are bringing mindfulness into the workplace.

You might expect to see mindfulness programs at Silicon Valley companies such as Apple, Facebook, eBay, Google, Twitter, and Yahoo. But more traditional companies such as Hughes Aircraft, General Mills, Abbott Laboratories, General Motors, Ford Motor Co., Time Warner Inc., Reebok, Xerox, IBM, Safeway Inc., Proctor & Gamble, Texas Instruments Inc., and Goldman Sachs are also embracing mindfulness programs. Naturally, teaching mindfulness

to business leaders—"mind fitness corporate training" as it's sometimes called—is, in itself, a growth industry.

Professor Bill George of Harvard Business School spoke with HuffPost Live about mindfulness and said that major companies like Google and General Mills are "really getting on board" and training employees in mindfulness practices. "Mindfulness," he says, "is the way to get out of this 24/7 stress-based world we're in." In fact, Sheryl Sandberg, chief operating officer at Facebook, admits that she meditates 5 minutes a day.

And it's not just corporate executives jumping on the mindfulness bandwagon. A quick search on Amazon.com for "meditation books," reveals 82,405 titles for sale, yet "meditation, all departments" lists 483,672 items, including books, CDs, DVDs.

WE ARE FAMOUS

Yet we are talking about conscious awakening.

Russell Brand has not shied away from discussing the importance of connection and the fact that we aren't just material beings. He wants to bring the people together to create a Consciousness Revolution.

Jim Carrey, one of our generation's funniest men, often speaks about consciousness and spirituality, and what it feels like to be awakened. He is also very active in the anti-vaccine movement. Carrey speaks of unknowingly being on a spiritual journey and what it was like to find oneself when he was a kid.

Billy Corgan, founder and lead vocalist for The Smashing Pumpkins, has been voicing his opinions about politics and the noticeable spiritual awakening that's happening all around the world. You can hear the deep understanding he has of what it means to be awakened in one of his interviews, and how society is being brainwashed into believing that material social status is more important than feeding our spirit with love and compassion for others.

Joe Rogan, comedian, actor, host and Ultimate Fighting Championship commentator, often talks about what he has learned from his awakening experiences. He hosts a podcast show called "The Joe Rogan Experience" where he talks about the mysteries of the world, politics, and changes we need to make to improve our lives and the lives of others around us.

Shirley MacLaine is an iconic actress who has been voicing her thoughts about spirituality, aliens, and making contact with otherworldly beings in a transcendental sense for decades. Her books, Out on a Limb and The Camino: A Journey of the Spirit, talk about her personal experiences from living the Hollywood lifestyle to the humbling aspects and practices of spirituality, which MacLaine says, "every human being should get to discover and understand and reflect upon."

WE ARE ANONYMOUS CONSUMERS

Yet we are influencing brands and other consumers' purchasing decisions.

Celebrities aren't the only ones influencing brands. Even anonymous consumers can have an impact on purchasing decisions. Consumer boycotts, for instance, have a long and noble history of contributing to progressive social change as well as succeeding in their more immediate goals to change consumer behaviors.

Here are a few examples.

PepsiCo will begin to make diet Pepsi products without aspartame later this year due to customer concerns about the safety of the artificial sweetener.

SodaStream closed its factory in the illegal Israeli settlement of Mishor Adumim following a high profile boycott campaign against the company. Major retailers in the United States and Europe, including Macys and John Lewis, pulled SodaStream from their shelves, and SodaStream was forced to close a flagship store in Brighton, England, because of pickets outside the store.

Good Energy in Wiltshire, England, dropped G4S as its meter reading contractor following consumer complaints about ethics. G4S is one of the largest security firms in the world and it is believed to be involved in human rights abuses and violations of international law through the security and custodial services it provides to the Israeli Occupation Forces.

Johnson & Johnson removed chemicals from its baby products after laboratory testing by the Campaign for Safe Cosmetics, a nonprofit watchdog group, revealed that its baby shampoo contained the carcinogen formaldehyde.

In France, Babybel was forced to apologize and withdraw products after disability groups called for a boycott of its cheese because the company ran a marketing campaign that used the phrase "mentally ill holidays."

Flannels, the United Kingdom's largest independent luxury retail group, stopped selling fur products after a targeted boycott by activists around the country,

DaitoCrea, a Japanese distributor of products made by Ahava Dead Sea Laboratories, stopped distributing Ahava products after a two-year boycott of its products. The decision was the direct result of a concerted campaign by the Palestine Forum Japan to educate Japanese consumers about Ahava's practices.

Values of the Consciousness Revolution

Now that we have a better understanding of who is in the Consciousness Revolution --and that we might be part of this revolution ourselves -- let's discuss the values that unite us by looking at brands that are thriving and why.

Few companies have awoken to this shift, and even though the following campaigns align with Consciousness Revolution values, that is likely due to coincidence rather than the brands' full understanding of this phenomenon.

WE ARE PROUD

We do not conform

The era of wearing clothing embellished with a logo has ended. Consumers are no longer interested in wearing T-shirts bearing a brand's logo. In fact, Abercrombie & Fitch has reduced branded clothing in its North American stores to nearly zero. The reason for the shift: The brand, which was a favorite among teens in the 1990s, noticed that personal style, especially among teens, is becoming less about fitting in and more about standing out.

Take-away for marketers: As demonstrated by Abercrombie & Fitch, this is the time for brands to embrace all cultures and backgrounds or get left behind.

WE ARE SELF-ACCEPTING

We challenge the status quo

Dove launched the Campaign For Real Beauty in 2004 to help women build a positive self-image and self-esteem. In 2013, Dove recruited seven women of different ages and backgrounds, and invited FBI-trained forensic artist Gil Zamora to create composite sketches of them based
on a stranger's description of them. Most of the women described themselves in a more negative way than the strangers described them. The campaign received praise from both industry experts and consumers. It articulates the way our society increasingly expects brands to stand by our side as we challenge the status quo.

Take-away for marketers: Authenticity is essential to any brand. Ultimately, we want to be at peace with who we truly are and not try to be someone we aren't just to please others. We also expect brands to be authentic as we become more true to ourselves.

WE WANT TO REACH OUR FULL POTENTIAL

We create communities

Reebok's new brand campaign, "Be More Human" is described as a rally cry for its consumers, urging them to live up to their full potential. The campaign is the culmination of a re-branding campaign that Reebok began five years ago when it started aligning itself with challenging exercise brands such as Cross Fit. This integrated marketing and advertising campaign gives consumers a challenge they can choose to accept and creates a loyal community of fans.

Take-away for marketers: Being our best self is one of the top values of the Consciousness Revolution. We want to see how far we can go, and social media has leveled the playing field, creating an opportunity for anyone to rise to the top.

WE ARE EMOTIONAL CONSUMERS

We like to feel positive

In a recent article, L'Oreal described a shift in its ad strategy that creates an emotional connection with its consumers instead of highlighting its products. Tying the famous "Because You're Worth It" tagline to a positive emotion helps create a genuine connection with the brand thus inspiring customer loyalty. Emotions are powerful. Brands that can capture emotions can connect and engage with customers.

Take-away for marketers: Consumers are emotional beings first and foremost. Tap into their feelings and emotions, and help them feel positive, happy, and good about themselves, and you will have a loyal customer.

How Do You Create an Awakened Brand?

The benefits of creating a brand that taps into the Consciousness Revolution are enormous. By connecting with the values and beliefs of your customers and employees, you are creating a legion of loyal brand ambassadors.

When you increase your brand's emotional connection with your customers, they will advocate for and defend your brand. When you strengthen your brand's relationship with your employees, they will feel more connected to your brand and your company.

Here are several actionable steps that will help transform your brand into an Awakened Brand.

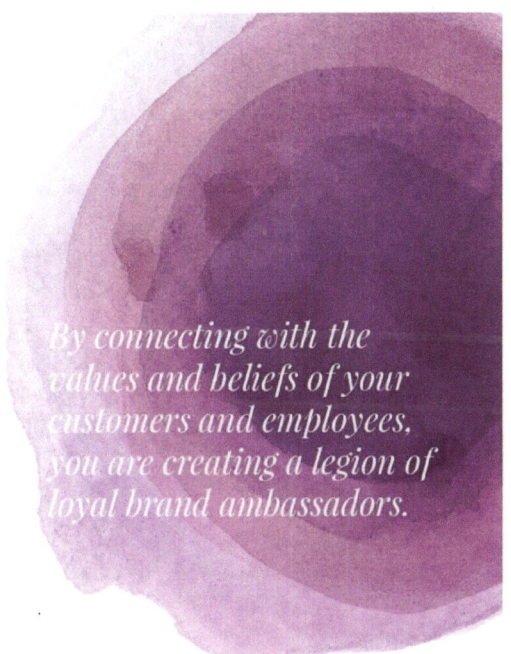

By connecting with the values and beliefs of your customers and employees, you are creating a legion of loyal brand ambassadors.

1. CHOOSE YOUR BRAND VALUES

Your executive team needs to go back to the origin of your brand and ask "why." Why are we making cereal, why are we providing insurance to people, why are we lending money to businesses? The answers need to come from your core team.

You, and your executive team, need to know what defines you as a brand and what you value as a team for others to connect with your brand. Your brand reflects the way customers perceive you. A good brand doesn't just happen. It requires a well-thought out, strategic plan, and it starts with your core values and beliefs.

These values are the DNA of your company. They align your employees to your brand, and help them create consistent messaging about everything from products to customer service.

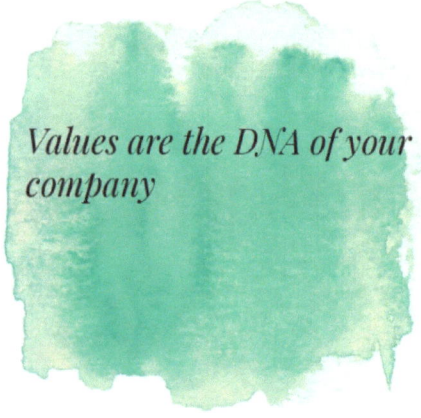

Values are the DNA of your company

Great Eastern Energy (GEE), is a provider of electricity and gas in the Northeast region that has been in the energy commodities business for the last 17 years.

We believe our role is to educate individuals and businesses on ways to save energy by consuming less of it. We want to help people change their behaviors around energy consumption. At GEE, we care about this issue deeply and it translates into every business decision we make, from creating products to developing advertising campaigns.

Patagonia is another company with a deep understanding of its brand's values. Patagonia knows what it is, what it values and what it stands for. Its mission statement is absolutely clear: "Build the best product, cause no unnecessary harm, use business to inspire and implement solutions to the environmental crisis."

Patagonia and its Founder Yvon Chouinard use the brand to educate and connect with its customers. In 2005, it started "The Cleanest Line," a blog that focuses on environmental issues that resonate with its outdoor enthusiast customers. The brand is willing to take political stances, something an overwhelming majority of brands try to avoid. During the last mid-term election, Patagonia ran a campaign, "I Vote for the Environment", that encouraged customers to register to vote and learn about candidates' environmental records in an effort to persuade its customers to vote for the most environmentally minded candidates.

The brand promoted the hashtag #becauseilove and encouraged people to tweet why and how they are voting for the environment.

"We have a mission to solve problems in the world," says Joy Howard, Patagonia's vice president of marketing. "That's very much a part of how we engage with consumers."

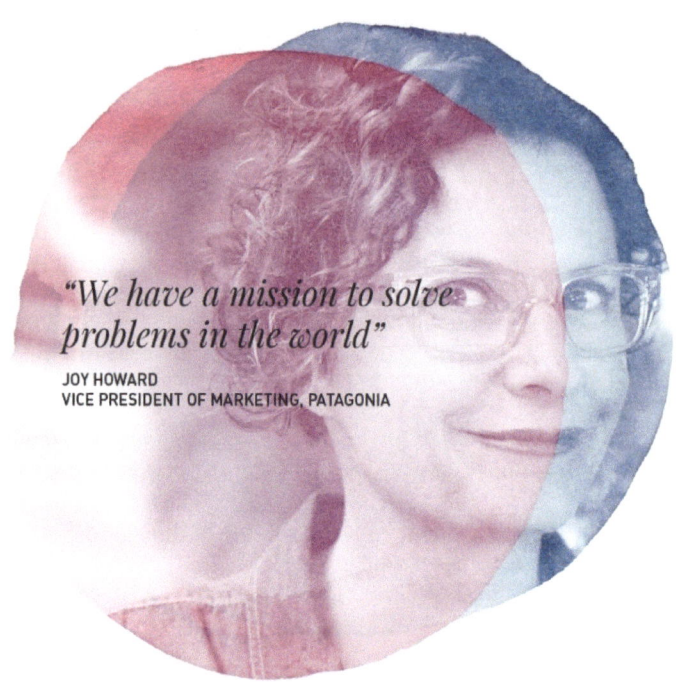

"We have a mission to solve problems in the world"

JOY HOWARD
VICE PRESIDENT OF MARKETING, PATAGONIA

2. CHOOSE YOUR CUSTOMER'S EMOTIONAL EXPERIENCE

Awakened Brands connect emotionally with their customers. The purpose and benefits of their brand, not just its features, are clearly identified so consumers can relate to the brand and its values. Once your brand values are clear, you can then connect with your customers' emotions.

The ability to connect your brand with customer's emotions requires your executive team to look beyond profits and the bottom line. The Consciousness Revolution asks leaders to be open-minded and emotional in their business decisions. In other words, if you want to be part of this revolution, you need to be bold and willing to explore unchartered territory.

At GEE, our teams focus on two emotions - inspiration and empowerment. We inspire our customers to learn more about energy consumption and change their behaviors, and we empower them by providing the tools and knowledge to act. Last year, to celebrate Earth Day (April 22), we shared 30 tips for reducing energy consumption in our daily lives. We want to inspire our customers to make a difference in our world through small changes that add up to big impacts.

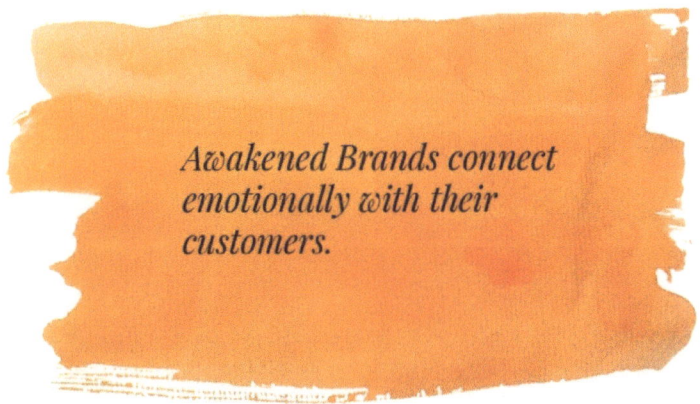

Awakened Brands connect emotionally with their customers.

We are also focusing on these emotions – to inspire and to empower -- internally. We've inspired our employees to be more positive by asking them to read and discuss, The Energy Bus, a book by Jon Gordon, which reveals 10 secrets for approaching life and work with positive energy that leads to true accomplishment at work and at home.

Lastly, we've empowered our employees to better understand each other through the Myers Briggs Assessment. This helps remove some of the communication challenges typically found in the workplace by giving us the tools to understand our colleagues' personalities. For instance, an introvert may not share the same excitement as an extravert but they will be as engaged with a project.

At the office, emotions can have a huge impact on employees' overall morale, productivity, and job performance. Positive emotions can create a positive work environment while negative emotions can lead to a negative work environment.

Positive emotions in the workplace can also improved employee health, reduce absenteeism, and increase job success due to an overall improvement in cognitive functions and psychological health. All emotions -- whether positive or negative -- are

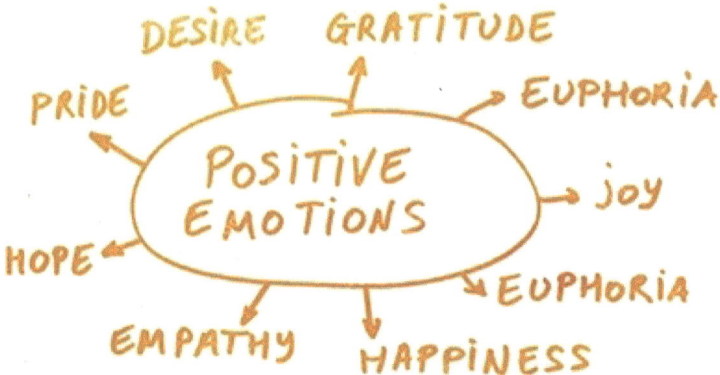

contagious. For example, a happy, prideful employee who is helpful will encourage other employees to act the same way. Positive emotions spread through teams and influence coworkers, and the end result is increased cooperation and an excellent job performance.

Associate your company and brand with positive emotions, and your employees and customers will want to share your brand with their family, friends, and colleagues. Your employees will feel better connected to your brand, and your customers will defend and advocate for your brand. In fact, happiness can affect your consumers' level of trust.

Happiness also is the main driver of social media sharing. An analysis of the IPA dataBANK, which contains 1,400 case studies of successful advertising campaigns, shows that ad campaigns with purely emotional content perform about twice as well (31% vs. 16%)

as those with only rational content and even outperformed ads that mixed emotional and rational content.

3. ENGAGE YOUR CUSTOMERS

Social media and technology have created opportunities for businesses to engage with consumers like never before. Today we see many brands forced to interact with customers online. But this is also an opportunity for businesses to take those interactions to the next level with co-creation and responsive storytelling framework.

CO-CREATION STRATEGY

We need customers to become more than evangelists or advocates for our brands. We need them to become co-creators and participate in product innovation.

Co-creation is a core value of the Consciousness Revolution. Consumers are no longer passive. They know what they want and they want to have a say in the products being created by companies. Ignoring consumers will kill your brand. Companies not communicating with their customers are like couples that don't communicate daily. Some people think co- creation is a Millennial concept and expectation but it's actually a trend across all generations.

Co-creation helps your company to meet customer needs while spending less money on product development and lowering the risks associated with bringing a new product to the marketplace because you are hearing firsthand what your customers want and need from your products. Think of co-creation as community problem solving.

Allowing consumers to co-create isn't always an easy concept for CEOs to grasp: It requires bravery to put faith in voices beyond the office walls.

The brand is willing to take political stances, something an overwhelming majority of brands try to avoid. During the last mid-term election, Patagonia ran a campaign, "I Vote for the Environment," that encouraged customers to register to vote and learn about candidates' environmental records in an effort to persuade its customers to vote for the most environmentally minded candidates.

The brand promoted the hashtag #becauseilove and encouraged people to tweet why and how they are voting for the environment.

"We have a mission to solve problems in the world," says Joy Howard, Patagonia's vice president of marketing. "That's very much a part of how we engage with consumers."

By giving your customers the opportunity to co-create, you're automatically encouraging brand loyalty. By becoming directly involved with your brand, your customers gain a feeling of influence and control, while seeing that their input actually matters, which encourages them to continue to engage.

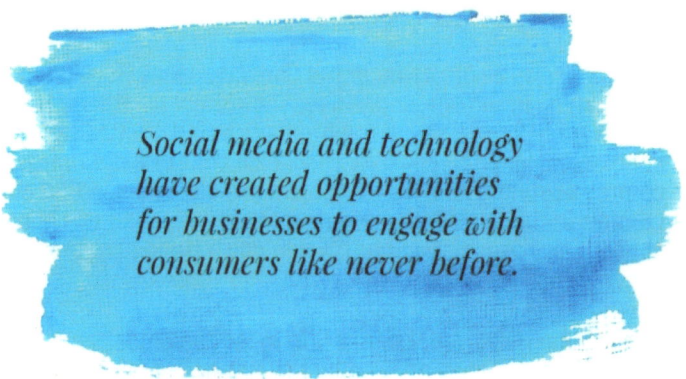

Social media and technology have created opportunities for businesses to engage with consumers like never before.

These brands have successfully used co-creation to develop their products.

- Ideas Brewery - Heineken idea brewery. Create the next great beer experience.

- My Starbucks Idea - Submit ideas for Starbucks products or community initiatives.

- GE Ecomagination - Submit ideas for environmentally friendly products.

- Kraft - Crowdstorming product ideas with Kraft.

Other well-known brands – from FedEx to General Electric – are taking crowdsourcing to new levels with co-creation. Here are some notable examples of co-creation that were highlighted in the Financial Post.

Problem: How to ensure on time, zero-defect delivery of live tissues for organ donation.
Solution: With external medical staff and suppliers, FedEx developed a sophisticated logistics technology that manages key variables like location, temperature, and pressure.

Problem: How to improve the performance of a call center.
Solution: Working with customers and call center agents, Microsoft redesigned the customer experience to make it more personal and responsive.

Problem: How to extract Alberta's heavy oil in an environmentally friendly, low-cost way.
Solution: GE, government officials, and customers collaborated at a shared innovation center to develop a new water filtration system that reduced water consumption.

RESPONSIVE STORYTELLING FRAMEWORK

Responsive storytelling is also essential to capturing your audience's attention. When communicating about your brand it is important you tell your brand's story in a way that is uniquely useful to each individual consumer. Instead of just telling your brand's story, tell your customer why your brand is relevant to them and how it will improve their lives.

As we saw before, the Consciousness Revolution has infused a strong desire in customers to be responsible and to thrive. They want to be involved in product creation because it fulfills their desire to influence products and to purchase products that improve our environment and society. It also gives customers the feeling that they are thriving and expanding their own capabilities and awareness.

The three key questions you need to answer when designing a responsive storytelling framework for your brand are:

What are you trying to accomplish?

Who is your audience?

Why should they care?

Create a responsive framework that lets your audience determine how the story of your brand is told.

Simple technology features such as breadcrumbs and smart user-driven navigation are essential to help guide the user through a story that he or she will co-create by allowing them to customize the content and interact with information presented in interactive infographics, charts, and maps.Consumers who want to take a deeper dive can rearrange the information and create their own unique experience, allowing your executive team to see how the information is being used and rearranged, giving them a better sense of what your customers value.

Some examples of this technology include Bloomberg Visual Data, which offers unlimited functionality, interactivity, and data integration. There are also more traditional options such as interactive PowerPoint, Prezi, and Google Slides that are a bit more restrictive but may be more accessible to consumers. Choose the technology that works best for your audience and resources, but remember that there are many ways to tell your story.

Whichever technology you choose, responsive storytelling will keep customers engaged longer. The key is to create a valuable experience for them that allows them to create a unique narrative that reinforces your credibility, and instills trust in you, your message, and your brand.

Responsive storytelling will keep customers engaged longer.

4. HIRE FOR ATTITUDE, TRAIN FOR SKILL

Great brands have a rigorous hiring process that allows them to hire employees who understand, support and champion the company culture. You can always train someone on new tools and processes but you can't change who they are. And who they are, their values, and their personality will affect your brand.

To implement successful co-creation and responsive framework tactics, your brand needs leaders who are willing to rethink their leadership style. Business author and adviser Tom Asacker says it perfectly: "Leaders are Sherpas. The root of the word 'lead' means 'to go forth, to travel.' Great leaders are simply great guides on other people's trips."

Great leaders trust others, which starts with trusting themselves. To create an Awakened Brand, it is crucial for all members of the executive team to remove all ego and fear, and let consumers participate in brand co-creation and innovation. The Author writes, Successful organizations are "... led by humble and hopeful leaders. Human beings who seek to learn and grow."

In "Why you hate work", Tom Asacker gives the perfect definition of leadership: "A leader's job is to paint an inspiring picture of the future. To help people align their skills and passions around getting to that destination. And to help them feel engaged, safe and supported during the journey."

Marketing is no longer the job of one person or one department within a company. Instead, the entire organization is responsible for marketing, and the marketing department should be renamed the Customer Department because marketing is all about customer engagement and tapping into your customer's emotions and desires.

Rather than a Chief Marketing Officer, companies creating an Awakened Brand need to hire a Chief Customer Technologist Officer to bridge the gap between the Marketing (Customer) Department and IT Department. These departments need to work hand-in-hand to engage and interact with customers using social media and technology.

"You can always train someone on new tools and processes but you can't change who they are."

TOM ASACKER

GROWTH HACKERS

"Growth Hacker" is a new type of marketer. While "Growth Hacker" may be a new term for most, it is a long-held practice among the best Internet marketers and product managers in Silicon Valley.

Growth hacking is the intersection between marketing and technology, says George Deeb. It's all about tracking and testing every way your brand relates to your customers online -- web page design, email, purchasing process, social media sharing links, website analytics, content, search engine optimization, landing pages, etc., and continually testing and improving it until you have that "Aha Moment" that leads to "rapid, viral and affordable customer growth." A growth hacker lives at the intersection of data, product and marketing, and finds a strategy within the parameters of a scalable and repeatable method for growth, driven by the product and inspired by data.

Because of growth hacking, it's now possible for new products and services to go from having zero users to 10 million users in just a few years. Previously, marketing relied on expensive, traditional communication channels such as newspaper and television advertising, and public relations and advertising agencies to spread the work about their products and services. The marketing department would send executives to conferences to give keynote speeches about their products and services. Today, companies can reach 10 million users for a fraction of the cost using technology and social media.

AGILE MARKETERS

Transforming your brand into an Awakened Brand also means that your marketing team is agile and willing to change and evolve with your customers' desires. Agile marketing is not only a process but also a mindset.

Agile marketing follows the same principles as Agile Development, often used to develop software. These principles are: respond to change, try rapid iterations, focus on testing and data, conduct numerous small experiments, and value collaboration. Agile marketing responds to customer's desires quickly and easily by improving the speed, predictability, transparency, and adaptability of the Marketing Department.

Testing an advertising campaign doesn't take three months anymore. It takes three days. Agile marketers start with projects that have a small reach and budget, and test them for a few days. They look at the engagement number, readjust the campaign, and test them again.

They repeat this again and again, and then invest in the campaigns that demonstrated the highest ROI. Going Agile allows Spotify to be faster, better, and cheaper than industry Goliaths like Google, Amazon, and Apple.

An agile marketer sets up different goals and objectives by driving long-term marketing strategies with short-term, customer- focused iterative projects that improve the responsiveness and relevance of the final product. Agile marketing allows for faster and more creative testing, smarter improvements, and better final results.

In addition to better final products, agile marketing also leads to more engaged employees. Employees working in agile environments report a greater overall sense of satisfaction and pride in their work due to feeling more empowered, greater clarity in how their role impacts the business, and a more collaborative work environment.

Our Journey

This is an exciting time to be in marketing. We have an opportunity to look closely at our brands' value and its promise and thereby create a deeper connection with our customers by engaging them to help us improve our products.

Leadership is the key to building an Awakened Brand. Our executive teams have to be willing to be bold and look beyond and think about personal values and how those values connect to the brand's values. We have to ask ourselves: Is marketing about generating revenue or is it about creating a value that will be exchanged for revenue?

Here are a few goals for our journey to creating an Awakened Brand:

We need to transform our Marketing Department into a Customer Service Department and expect our teams to become technology savvy and product driven.

We need executive board members to care more about the well-being of employees than the value of their stock.

We need CEOs to refuse their golden package when employees are being laid off.

We need politicians to have a vision of how they can improve our society and not just a vision about their career.

And we need marketers to be connected with their emotions and values, and to be sitting right next to CEOs when companies are making important decisions about values, brands, and what customers truly desire.

It is urgent to define our own life values, and while we are at it, to define our brand's ethics and promises. Do they align? Are they in competition? How can we align your brand with our own values?

We don't need more products, we need better products. We don't need more customers; we need better-engaged customers who are co-creators of our brands.

This is the job of all Departments. This is our job.

Share with me your experience and feedback at
virginieglaenzer@hotmail.com

-- VIRGINIE GLAENZER

ACKNOWLEDGEMENTS

I owe a special debt of gratitude to Lisa Roepe and Krasimir Galabov for their inspired teamwork. Thank you to Emily Verner, Director of Digital Marketing at Great Eastern Energy, for her support and contribution. A special thank you to Tom Asacker for his generosity and trust. Finally, I would like to thank my husband Eric Glaenzer for his unconditional support.

LISA ROEPE

Freelance Writer

KRASIMIR GALABOV

Graphic Designer

One way I stay aware and conscious is by writing metaphysical poems. It relaxes my mind and helps me breath slowing and deeply.

Silomene ebooks and paperback books, available on Amazon.

www.ingramcontent.com/pod-product-compliance
Lightning Source LLC
Chambersburg PA
CBHW040917180526
45159CB00002BA/502

* 9 7 8 1 5 1 7 7 7 5 5 4 4 *